Organising Idea No. 3

A monograph published for the
EUROPEAN THERAPY STUDIES INSTITUTE

To our families, friends and colleagues,
and all the clients from whom
we have learnt so much.

Breaking the cycle of depression:
a revolution in psychology

© Joseph Griffin & Ivan Tyrrell 2000
Second edition © Joseph Griffin & Ivan Tyrrell 2000
Third edition © Joseph Griffin & Ivan Tyrrell 2002

HG Publishing for the
European Therapy Studies Institute
Chalvington, Hailsham, East Sussex BN27 3TD, United Kingdom

Printed in Great Britain

ISBN 1 899398 01 5

Breaking the cycle of depression:

a revolution in psychology

Joseph Griffin & Ivan Tyrrell

"Everything has now changed, except for our way of thinking."

Albert Einstein (d.1955)

"New organs of perception come into being because of necessity.
So, necessitous one, increase your need."

Jallaludin Rumi (d.1273)

Organising Ideas

"All scientific knowledge is a correlation of *what* is seen with the *way* that it is seen."

Henri Bortoft, *The Wholeness of Nature*

In all fields confusion flourishes, mistakes are made and harm is done when we forget that the *way* we look at phenomena is dependent on an active effort of imagination and thinking. We are not mechanical recording instruments looking out on a fixed world (although this is certainly the philosophy of science which is usually communicated by the way science is taught in schools, presented in popular books and revealed in television programmes). We *organise* what we see through what we believe we know.

When a field of study is confused about something, it usually needs a new organising idea.

An organising idea plays an active role in shaping our perception, thinking and research and is always larger than earlier ideas because it has to explain the anomalies that previously caused confusion.

This paper, one of a series commissioned by the European Therapy Studies Institute, offers a new organising idea.

ETSI 2002

"Bury me in the earth on which I suffered."

Extract from a suicide note

"Take a sad song and make it better."

Lennon and McCartney

Breaking the cycle of depression:
a revolution in psychology

LIVING with a depressed person is difficult. You have to work hard to protect yourself from being sucked into their deeply miserable and barren world view, devoid as it is of all the stimuli that make life interesting and pleasurable. Lifting depression, by contrast, is one of the most satisfying and enjoyable aspects of working as a counsellor or psychotherapist. Moreover, when you understand how and why clinical depression occurs, and employ treatment techniques which take account of this, it's easy to do – *and* you can help most people quickly. Using human givens therapy, for example, it often takes fewer than six sessions to lift even severe cases.

Depression is now the number one psychological disorder presenting in the Western world.[1] Epidemiological studies have shown that the rate of increase of depression has grown in all age groups. It is growing fastest in young people.[2] And suicide rates have increased in all countries, especially among the young.[3] The population born since 1945 has seen depression increase by a factor of nearly ten since their grandparents' time.[4] And this rate is accelerating. In just four years between 1994 and 1998 the number of people seeking help from their GPs for depression in the UK rose from four million to nine million (although some of this increase may have been due to the de-stigmatising of the condition in the media, encouraging more people to come forward for help).[5]

Furthermore, as countries become westernised, their rates of depression increase. The World Health Organisation (WHO), in the report *The global burden of disease,* estimates that depression will be second only to ischaemic heart disease as a cause of injury and disease worldwide by the year 2020.[6]

Defining depression

Depression is an emotion – a very *strong* emotion – and a depressive is someone who is highly emotionally aroused. The word 'arousal' may feel unfamiliar when linked with depression. However, even though depressed people often look 'flat' and inactive, the levels of the stress hormone cortisol in their blood are much higher than normal.[7]

Because women are, on average, much more in tune and responsive to their emotional life, higher rates of depression in women are to be expected. And this is what we find. Between 2.3% – 3.2% of men are diagnosed as depressed and 4.5% to 9.3% of women. Thus the rate of depression in women is two to three times higher. This is not simply due to differential reporting but to the different biological, sociological and psychological pressures on women.[8]

If we look at the rate of lifetime occurrences of depression the same pattern holds. The chance of developing a major depression is one in ten in men and one in four in women. In addition, women on average take 50% longer to recover spontaneously from depression.[9]

So what do emotions do? All emotions – anger, hate, fear, love, greed (in all its forms) and sexual desire, hypnotically lock us in to a confined viewpoint – which we refer to as focusing attention.[10] Whilst in the grip of *any* powerful emotion, we can be said to be in an emotionally driven trance state. Depression is no exception.[11]

Our emotional responses arise from the limbic system, often called the emotional brain, and are all connected in some way to the basic survival instincts we share with every other mammal. It is because they are concerned with survival that they are so powerful and easily override our reasoning mind, the brain's higher cortex, which, in evolutionary terms, is a comparatively recent development. This means that we must always be prepared for an emotional hijack when the limbic system believes its survival is threatened or its needs are not being met.[12]

Emotions which lock us into a confined viewpoint, by 'focusing our attention' in a trancelike state, can as easily be stimulated by thoughts – imagination – as by real events. The importance of this will become clear shortly.

Like all emotions, depression conveys a two-way message: to the people around the emotional person, and to the individual concerned.

The message the depressed individual is sending is, "I am stuck, I am blocked in my life, I don't know where to go from here".

For most of our existence human beings lived in small, cohesive tribal groups, so when somebody gave out that message, it was readily identified. The group would understand how and why the person was blocked *and be able to do something about it.*

In traditional, so called primitive, non-westernised societies, and a few still survive, depression is almost unknown. Such people live in cohesive communities where they are kept busy with meaningful activity and where practical problems are dealt with quickly. Studies of traditional New Guinea tribes or the Amish community, for example, which still tries to live a seventeenth century lifestyle, show that if a hut or barn burns down, everyone rallies round to rebuild it straight away. There is community support for individuals, balanced by an understanding that the individual has a responsibility to the community.[13] But depression always increases in third world countries when they become unstable due to rising uncertainty caused by political violence, population increase, food shortages etc.[14]

Our modern technological society is an increasingly complex and stressful culture where more and more people find it difficult to get their emotional needs met. Today a person can send out an emotional message for months or years, and nobody may actually notice or, if they do, they will lack the collective wisdom to do anything about it.

Reasons for the increase in depression

Modern living takes its toll in many ways which help account for the big increase in depression. Here are some of the most important of them.

Technology/consumerism:

In technologically advanced societies, the loosening of social structures has increased the pattern of family and community breakdown. Modern communications technology plays a big role in this. The media in a consumerist society increasingly emphasise the acquisition of material goods and place more emphasis on the 'me', with a decreasing lack of commitment to other people and to wider social responsibilities. This can encourage an obsessional preoccupation with the self with which depression is linked.

It is normal for toddlers to scream "I want it now!" As far as they are concerned they are at the centre of the Universe. In healthy families, as children grow, they are taught to have a more realistic expectation of how things happen. They learn that people have to wait their turn, that success in life is earned, that wants are not the same as needs, that the needs of others should be considered and that they themselves are *not* the centre of the Universe. But, in this consumerist age, it suits many vested interests to keep as much of the population as possible in the selfish six-year-old stage by undermining this healthy developmental process.

"Take the waiting out of wanting" (the same thought that drives psychopaths) was the famous advertising slogan used to launch credit cards in the UK. Television programmes and the advertisements that surround them, coupled with corresponding peer group pressure, raise expectations in the population. These expectations stimulate in many a desire for the 'good' life NOW, as if it were a right, undermining the necessity for learning, work and patience in due proportion.

The media also imbue people with simplified thoughts about how we should educate children, what we should wear, how much attention we should get, what love is and what we should enjoy and be moved by. Many people are unable to step aside from the influences of the entertainment and advertising industries which constantly assail us, cleverly stimulating our greed, and thus manipulating the way we live our lives.

Time pressures:

While technology can clearly remove pressures, it can also creates new ones. Since the invention of the mechanical clock we have increasingly broken days down to hours and minutes and driven ourselves by this artificial measurement. The consequence is that we pack more into the day and organise the way we cooperate with one another more efficiently. This brilliant innovation made industrialisation and modern, organised society possible, but it has also brought many subtle problems with it, not least an increase in time related stress. It tends to leave, for example, no time for spontaneous relaxation.

This has more serious consequences than might at first be apparent. When we are driven by the clock we ignore our own, highly evolved and infinitely subtle internal biological clocks – our natural ultradian rhythms.[15] It is quite normal to 'switch off' for twenty minutes every hour and a half as the brain swaps hemispherical dominance from left to right in order to process information, lay long term memories down and do internal mental and physical repair work. Indeed we are designed to do this and, whenever we override our natural need for a twenty-minute break, it always involves the production of stress hormones to keep us alert. If we continually and inappropriately override our need for regular relaxation in the workplace and become highly stressed, we become mentally unstable and, eventually, physically ill.[16]

Many people now find it difficult to wind down without the instant application of TV, music, drugs or alcohol to change mood. The ubiquitous presence of TV and computers in the home increasingly restricts the amount of time children spend talking amongst themselves and with their parents – which steadily retards their social skills development.

Another time related stressor is our heightened expectation for instant solutions to every problem. Enormous amounts of information are now available cheaply and easily through computers and the internet, but there has been no corresponding mental and emotional education in how to discern the usefulness and meaning of the information. This leads many to feel an emptiness of purpose in life.

Uncertainty:

Consider for a moment some of the changes in workplace practices that unsettle us. There is a widely perceived sense of uncertainty and injustice in the world about job stability, which has been generated by technological development and the ease with which capital investment in industry and commerce can move around the world, ruthlessly seeking a better deal. This is often cited as a cause of stress and depression. Certainly short-term employment contracts have become the norm in professions where one used to consider one could 'have a job for life'. Increasingly, too, redundancy and the lesser likelihood of getting another job, particularly after the age of 40, are decreasing self esteem and creating the mental and physical burden of financial difficulty and debt. Control over how we work and live is slipping from our grasp yet that sense of being in control is essential for mental stability and physical health.[17] We cannot handle too much change.

However, there is a paradox here. No human being has *ever* known what's around the corner. We all, in fact, live a transient life whilst pretending that life is constant. Being prepared for change is a positive attribute, minimising the risk of suffering stress reactions, anxiety, ill-health and worse when the inevitable changes happen.

Mobility:

Travel has never been easier, but we pay dearly for it in ways too numerous to mention here, other than to point to an example that relates directly to depression; that the ease with which it is now possible to move away, work and live elsewhere has contributed to the breakdown of close extended family support in times of trouble.

Relationship breakdown:

Research shows that children can be damaged more by the strife leading up to divorce and its subsequent effects than by the death of a parent.[18] For instance, in the UK, children of middle-class parents who were born in 1958 and whose parents divorced before they were sixteen were twice as likely to leave school without any qualifications as those whose parents remained married. They showed more behaviour problems in school, were more likely to be unhappy and worried, and were behind their schoolmates at reading and arithmetic. They were also much less likely to go to university or to be in a job when they were twenty-three years of age. They were four times more likely to live in subsidized social housing and were much more likely to smoke than were other middle-class people whose parents had not split up. They were on average also less emotionally stable, left home earlier and themselves divorced or separated more frequently later in life.[19] Such findings are significant because of the rapid growth in broken families we are seeing nowadays, throughout society.

Although single-parent families are now very common, life expectancy is higher, and physical and mental health are much better for mothers, fathers and children in two parent families. An enormous body of evidence shows that children from stable families grow up with fewer behavioural and emotional problems, are better socialised and less likely to drift into drugs and criminal behaviour than those who come from one-parent or divorced families. They also appear to make better parents themselves.[20]

It is still true that the majority of people can adapt and cope well, even with this large range of pressures, indeed we have evolved to be adaptable, but nevertheless many do not. The increasing rate of technological and social change is creating a more psychologically disturbed population. The rapid rise in anxiety disorders, depression, addictions and antisocial behaviour illustrates, reflects and compounds this trend.

Depression is not a genetic illness

The increase in the rate of depression revealed in epidemiological studies makes it clear that depression is not, in the main, a biological disease. Genes do not change that quickly. Despite the explosion in genetic research and gene mapping, and high hopes of finding a gene for everything, no 'depression gene' exists because genes don't work that way.[21]

Over the last three decades conclusive evidence has mounted to show that the vast majority of depressions are learned, created by the way we interact with our environment.[22] We now know that depression is not an event-driven phenomenon – it is not caused by specific events *per se*. The majority of people exposed to adverse life circumstances do not develop depression. The reaction of depression is caused by how individuals have learned to respond to adverse life experiences. We shall have more to say on this later.

Further support for the environmental or learned view of depression is the evidence that depression responds well to certain kinds of psychotherapeutic intervention.[23] Moreover, such interventions greatly reduce the rate of relapse compared to drug treatments based on the biological model. The brain is sufficiently conditionable by experiences, *and reconditionable,* that depressed people can be helped to adapt more effectively to the pressures and uncertainties of modern living, whatever their history. They can *learn* to respond to adverse life circumstances in better ways.

That there is a biological *component* to depression is undisputed since all our emotions are expressed in the language of biochemistry. Also, depression affects our biology by, for example, impairing our immune system. But the idea that depression is the result of a chemical imbalance in the brain, so disempowering and yet so fervently promoted by drug manufacturers, is wrong. It is now clear that changes in serotonin levels in the brains of depressives are a *consequence* of depression, not the *cause* of it. Serotonin levels fluctuate constantly and are directly correlated with the effectiveness with which we are living our lives. Life enhancing experiences raise serotonin levels at least as effectively as drugs and more instantaneously.

The accepted symptoms of clinical depression

The *Diagnostic and Statistical Manual of Mental Disorders* sets out the criteria for a major depressive episode.[24] When someone shows five or more of the following symptoms, including either one of the first two, for a two week period, they are considered to be suffering a major depression.

- Depressed mood
- Loss of pleasure or interest in usual activities
- Disturbance of appetite
- Sleep disturbance
- Psychomotor retardation or agitation
- Loss of energy
- Feelings of worthlessness and guilt
- Difficulties in thinking
- Recurrent thoughts of death or suicide.

The most effective approaches to treatment

The United States Public Health Service Agency, mandated in 1979 to provide guidelines for the treatment of depression, initiated a literature search from 1975–1990 which looked at some 100,000 pieces of research. Over 3,500 of the best studies were selected to form the guidelines and were peer reviewed by 73 professional societies including the British Psychiatric Society and the British Psychological Society.[25]

The guidelines for effective treatment are:

- Therapy should be active, time limited, focused on current problems and aimed at symptom resolution not personality change
- Psychotherapy should be considered the first line treatment approach if the depression is mild to moderate, if it is non-psychotic, not chronic, not highly recurrent and if the patient wants it
- Medication should be the first line treatment if the depression is very severe, if there have been two prior episodes, if there is a family history of depression and if the patient wants it.

This massive research programme quite clearly shows that the types of psychological treatment that are effective in lifting depression are brief, short term therapies such as interpersonal therapy, cognitive and behavioural therapy.

The least successful forms of psychotherapy are psycho-dynamic therapy and so-called 'insight' counselling – both of which may maintain and deepen depression. (The term 'insight' counselling is now generally associated with the methods of psychodynamic schools of therapy, although providing *true* insight into the patterns of how depression is created is an important part of any therapy.[26])

It is also well established that antidepressants can be effective in lifting the symptoms of clinical depression – completely in a third of those who take them and partially in another third – although they are not nearly as effective in preventing further episodes of depression as the right type of psychotherapy. Antidepressants don't work at all in a third of those who are prescribed them and for many people the side effects are more unpleasant than the depression so they stop taking them. It takes between four and six weeks for them to exert their maximum effect. There is, as yet, no widely accepted agreement for why antidepressants work when they do, although the placebo effect is known to play a part.[27]

Antidepressants are very powerful drugs and should rarely be used with children because their brains are still forming. (New research shows that the frontal lobe connections are not fully in place until a person is about 20 years old.[28]) Because of the toxic side effects often experienced they should also be cautiously prescribed to older people who have any sign of brain deterioration.

St John's wart (Hypericum), the most widely prescribed treatment in Germany for depression, has been shown to be as effective as antidepressants with fewer side effects.[29] It has also been used to help people with sleep disorders.[30] As with antidepressant drugs until now it has not been known why it works.[31]

Most experts now recommend a combination of medicine and psychotherapy but, since the US research was published, more and more studies show that medication is irrelevant if *appropriate* psychotherapy is given.[32]

On the basis of all the above information, we can now start to answer three vital questions.

1) What are the defining common links between depressions?

2) Why do some forms of therapy work and others not?

3) What is the most effective treatment approach to take?

The answers offered here emanate from the human givens approach to understanding and treating emotional disorders.

Depression and the human givens

The human givens approach looks at each person holistically using an understanding of the psychobiological tools and needs that human beings have evolved over millions of years to cope with their environment.[33] Human givens therapy looks for what is missing in patients' lives and works towards correcting this imbalance so needs are met. It uses a blend of the cognitive, behavioural and interpersonal approaches that are proven to be effective, plus other elements such as deliberately stimulating the imagination of patients. It clearly distinguishes *needs* from *wants* and builds on the resources inherent in the person to add to their cognitive, emotional and behavioural skills base where necessary. Therapists and counsellors who learn to work in this way appear to get lasting results with most of their patients very quickly.

One of the tools with which humans have been programmed is the ability to dream every night. A new understanding of why we dream has given us a key to what is happening with the depressed person, both on a psychological and a biological level.[34]

Dreaming and depression

Every night we dream during what is known as rapid eye movement (REM) sleep, so named after the physiological state in which the eyes dart about beneath the closed eyelids.

It has been known for some time that, if REM sleep is prevented by waking a depressed patient every time they begin to dream, severe depression often lifts.[35] (Unfortunately the depressed state returns once the person resumes normal sleeping, or may even worsen because of extra compensatory REM sleep, so this cannot be used as a treatment.)

It is also known that electroconvulsive therapy (ECT), despite its bad press, can and does lift depression but, up till now, there has been no explanation as to why. We do know, however, that ECT causes REM sleep deprivation by producing seizure-like stimulation of the brain's higher cortex. Unlike direct REM sleep deprivation, the lifting of depression with ECT has a lasting effect, even when normal sleep is resumed, because there is no compensatory REM sleep afterwards.

So why should reduction in REM sleep lead to a reduction in depression? The answer lies in how the visual brain stimulates itself in REM sleep. There is a mechanism in the brain which shows up in EEG recordings as a wave. It is known as the PGO wave because the signals that create it originate in a part of the brain called the pons (P) from the neurones that move the eyes and are then conducted to both the lateral geniculate (G) body in the thalamus and to the occipital cortex (O) – hence the term PGO wave. This wave is the orientation response that draws our attention to sudden changes in the environment, such as a loud bang or sudden movement, anything that focuses our attention. It evolved in mammals to activate the flight or fight response to potential danger and is the system which manages the body's responses to stress. But it is also part of the mechanism which focuses our attention *whenever needed* on *anything* that interests us.

During REM sleep, and just before it starts, there is a massive firing of the orientation response. We suggest that the reason the eyes dart about during REM sleep is that they are trying to scan the environment in response to this firing of the orientation response. The PGO wave is signalling, "there is something to look out for here", and so the eyes keep on trying to look, darting about in all directions behind closed eyelids. However, there is no information coming in from the external world. The source of the arousal is internal – the unexpressed emotional introspections from the previous day, major or minor, which are still occupying space in the brain. The act of dreaming, by metaphorically acting out those unresolved introspections, discharges those arousals and frees the brain to be ready for the concerns of the following day.

But what happens when the emotional arousal level is extreme, as in depressed and anxious people? Hundreds of studies have shown that the fight or flight stress response is hyperactive in severely depressed patients.[36] In other words, the morbid and prolonged introspection and self examination, which tends to characterise depressed people, leads to above normal levels of emotional arousal which then need to be discharged during their dreams. In fact, the pressure for emotional discharge caused by excessive negative introspection is so great that the first REM period of the night occurs much earlier in depressed people, is more prolonged and shows an especially high rate of discharge. This amount of discharge not only reduces the level of arousal in the brain but actually exhausts it, leaving the person more likely to lack motivation the next day. It is no wonder that so many depressed people say they wake up exhausted from a nights sleep.

As the early hours of the morning are when we have our longest period of dreaming, from this perspective the early morning awakening seen in many depressed people could be construed as the body's way of preventing any further discharge of arousal caused by excessive self analysis. In other words, the brain is trying to protect itself by waking early.

So, we suggest, depressed people are tired and lacking in energy when they wake up because their orientation response mechanism is overworked. It has fired off so much during excessive dream sleep that it is exhausted. And, without this response effectively alerting them to what is happening around them, and enabling them to switch attention from one thing to another, they find it very difficult, if not impossible, to motivate themselves to do anything.

This explains the common complaint of depressed people: that they feel that "everything is meaningless ... pointless ... not worth bothering about". It is a human given that, to feel fulfilled and mentally healthy, we need a sense of meaning and purpose in our lives. But depressed people no longer have the means to generate it because their attention switching mechanism is exhausted, leaving them unable to refocus on the bigger picture. It is a closed circle. Although the orientation response gradually recovers as the day goes on, typically the depressive now emotionally introspects on that feeling of emptiness, the tiredness, the lack of joy or enthusiasm, and is driven into another intense period of dreaming the following night – piling misery on misery – and becoming even more depressed.

Depression, we suggest, is a natural response to certain types of emotional introspection that result in excessive dreaming. There are clear therapeutic implications suggested by this new, holistic view of the causal sequence in depression.

The trigger factor for depression may be some experience of loss: redundancy, failed relationship, divorce, death of a loved one or a financial setback. If the person tends to be of a pessimistic disposition, this will lead to excessive negative emotional introspection about the loss, which in turns leads to an excess of emotional arousal discharge through the dream state. In a minority of cases, in a predisposed person, genetic influences may contribute to triggering an excess of negative introspections. But, in either case, the most long lasting benefit is likely to derive from psychological interventions that alleviate the negative introspections, particularly if they teach the depressed person how to do this for themselves.

And that is exactly the case. Research shows that such interventions are more effective than antidepressants in reducing
further episodes of depression.[37]

Why some people get depressed and others don't

Why do some people get locked into depression while others,
with equal or more hardship in their lives, do not? It is, of
course, natural to feel deep sadness or depression at times.
But it is what happens next and how individuals react to it
that is crucial. The emotional arousal of deep grief or sadness
forces the brain back into primitive black and white modes of
thinking. To the emotional brain everything is either good or
bad, right or wrong, safe or dangerous, happy or sad, perfect or
irretrievably imperfect. And when emotional arousal is maintained it diverts the higher cortex away from using its highly
evolved ability to tolerate ambiguity and consider the bigger
picture.

People who are not habitual black and white thinkers can
'snap' out of this arousal fairly quickly. However people who
have a tendency towards analysing what's gone wrong in their
lives, reviewing the past selectively (picking out the negative
aspects), catastrophising every little setback, dreaming up
future disasters or engaging in self-blame tend to become locked
into the state of depression instead of rising above it. This
explains something observed for some time – that depressed
people have a particular style of thinking they habitually adopt
to explain things that happen to and around them. This is
known as attributional style.[38]

We all have an inbuilt need to make sense of our world and
to explain to ourselves why things happen the way they do.
The type of explanation we give ourselves – our attributional
style – is critical and determines whether or not we will get
depressed when bad things happen to us.

The three most important variables determining our attributional style are:

• How *personally* we take events (Do we tend to blame ourselves for *every* setback rather than considering all other possible reasons for something going wrong? If a relationship breaks down, for example, is it always our fault?)

• How *pervasive* we view events to be (If we lose a job do we think our whole life is ruined or do we limit the damage to a short period of time and see that now there is the possibility that other career opportunities can open up?)

• How *permanent* we think an event is. (Whether we think a setback will be short lived or go on for ever. If we don't get the house we have set our heart upon, for example, do we say, "Oh well, perhaps something else even better will turn up," or "I will never be happy again as long as I live"?)

If we take things personally, interpret events as all pervasive or all encompassing and think setbacks last forever, we are candidates for depression. This is because these emotionally driven black and white thinking styles inevitably generate more emotion by repeatedly turning on the fight or flight response which makes us angry (fight) or anxious (flight). In other words, when people catastrophise the 'bad' things that happen to them, magnifying them so that the whole of their life is affected, they are either making themselves feel very hostile (anger), or frightening themselves (anxiety).

This excessive turning on of the fight or flight response, results in the 'all or nothing' reaction to life events found in all depressed people and explains why depressives find it difficult to break the whole down into relevant component parts. When thinking is driven by the emotional brain it cannot see the infinite shades of grey between different viewpoints. That is why so many depressives are perfectionists: if an event they anticipated didn't go totally as planned, for example, it was a disaster; if a relationship isn't perfect, it is terrible. This same tendency makes some depressives prone to excessive jealousy.

Most things that happen in life have multiple causes. When we are more objective we can see the truth of this and we don't have to blame ourselves unreasonably when things go wrong. But depressed people, because of their emotional arousal, are not able to think clearly. That is why they plump for the big, simple-minded, single cause to explain a setback. "Either I am to blame or somebody else is to blame." They either get unreasonably angry with someone else for their difficulties or see themselves as the cause of their difficulties, generating self blame and low self esteem. It has not been possible, up to now, to understand why antidepressant medication can help relieve chronically hostile feelings. But we can now see that *any* prolonged emotionally arousing introspection, including fear or anger, can lead to depression.

(Our increasingly litigious society, where people are encouraged to sue for every minor misfortune or accident, forcing the law to apportion blame and put a price on it, may also be a reflection of increasing psychological destabilisation.)

Healthy people are not driven by these emotional hijacks of the higher cortex. They know how to moderate the assessments they make as circumstances change. On the other hand, black and white thinkers often make lifelong fixed judgements. For example, a woman hurt when her partner left her might decide she will never embark on a relationship again. She thinks *all* men are untrustworthy, so her human need for intimacy is not met and she withdraws into herself.

Learning about all the shades of grey

A person's attributional style has been shown to be highly correlated with their parents' attributional style. This doesn't mean that depression is a genetically transmitted disease; it simply means that we tend to model our parents' emotional behaviour and corresponding thinking style. Personality research shows that genetics make a 50% contribution to our personality. This means, therefore, that 50% of our personality is environmentally determined. Good therapy involves working with the relationship between both, helping people use genetic traits (for example, a tendency towards obsessive attention to detail) in a positive rather than a negative way.

Because people who are prone to depression tend to perceive the difficulties that arise in life as permanent, they become pessimists. It takes considerable and consistent effort on the part of others to resist such a view. As a consequence it can spread. Whole families become pessimistic and depressed.[39]

Pessimism is a major risk factor for depression. Most people who are clinically depressed don't even go to their GPs because their pessimism convinces them that their situation is hopeless. They may go only because somebody has nagged them into it. This means that, when they *do* go for counselling, it is terribly important that the pessimism – the hopelessness – is challenged in the very first session. The whole session should *never* be given over to history-taking because the patient might not come back, or might even commit suicide, before the next appointment. It must be demonstrated in the first session that change is possible. This is summed up in the phrase coined by solution focused therapists: "Do something that makes a difference *today*".

But pessimism is not only a high risk factor for clinical depression, it is also a major risk factor for all kinds of illnesses later on in life. It is a bigger determinant or predictor of a shortened life-span than any other.[40]

We can now see why an important part of any therapist's skill is the ability to calm people's emotions down.[41] Only when they are no longer aroused by the emotion of depression can a patient begin to reason, analyse or imagine different scenarios sufficiently well to perceive that life is complex, that there are multiple reasons for why things happen and that their excessive self-blame, or anger at others, is unrealistic.

People who don't get depressed can see variations – the shades of grey. They have the ability to limit the damage done by a particular negative experience so that they can concentrate on the good parts of their life. They might think, for example, "It's terrible that I've lost this relationship, but other parts of my life are working. I've got a good job. I've got a family to support me. And, of course, I'm free to get into another relationship again in the future." Or they might say, "It was rotten luck that I had abusive parents – but I didn't choose the bed I was born in. I can see that other parents make a much better job of it than mine did and I'm going to use my experience to do better by *my* children."

Mentally healthy people are flexible thinkers who limit the damage of a setback by *not* globalizing. They recognise what is within their control and what is not. They don't get sucked into the illusion that they have *total* control in any situation, nor that they have none at all. This is the opposite of what depressives do.

When depressed people have a setback, they simplify it by dramatically exaggerating the hopelessness of the situation and the number of difficulties they have – catastrophic thinking. They may start blaming themselves. They emotionally introspect and, consequently, because of the excessive dreaming this causes, feel tired and so begin to progressively eliminate all sources of pleasurable stimulation from their lives. It becomes too much of an effort for them to go out and socialise, to exercise, make love, keep up their hobbies and interests or celebrate anything. Every time they back out of doing something pleasurable they feel a brief sense of relief and comfort, but they never make the connection to the fact that, a couple of hours later, they are even more depressed. And it's the progressive elimination of positive stimulation from their lives that drops them deeper into the black pit of despair.

To recap: depression is an emotion that simplifies (regresses) thinking patterns which, in turn, encourages emotionally arousing introspections that give rise to distorted REM sleep. This causes excessive dreaming which leaves the person drained of the energy they need for the normal arousal of attention, motivation and the drawing of meaning from their everyday activities. This theory accounts for all the symptoms of severe depression – depressed mood, loss of pleasure or interest in usual activities, disturbance of appetite, sleep disturbance, psychomotor retardation or agitation, loss of energy, feelings of worthlessness and guilt, difficulties in thinking, and recurrent thoughts of death or suicide. In other words, it explains the complete psychobiological cycle of depression.

Why some treatments work and others don't

The theory explains, for example, why antidepressants, though crude, work for many people. (All antidepressants either reduce REM sleep or are actively involved in the correction of the disordered REM sleep, bringing the pattern back to normal.[42]) The reason there is such a high rate of relapse when people stop taking the drugs, compared to effective psychotherapy or counselling, is because drugs can't meet unm,et emotional needs or change attributional thinking style. The theory also explains why any form of counselling or psychotherapy that encourages emotional introspection – Rogerian, analytical, psychodynamic, gestalt etc – is contraindicated for depressed people. (Unfortunately millions around the world have had their depressions maintained and more deeply entrenched by well meaning therapists working out of these models. Now American hospitals employing therapists using these outmoded models are being successfully sued for large sums of money by the relatives of depressed people.[43])

Equally the human givens approach explains why some therapeutic methods work so effectively. **Behaviour therapy** works, for example, because it guides the person back into doing enjoyable physical activities that take the focus off themselves, re-engaging them with the environment and pulling them away from negative introspecting. As the client takes up challenging and interesting activities again, mental or physical, this, in turn, stimulates an increase in serotonin levels which helps to regulate REM sleep.

"There is nothing either good or bad, but thinking makes it so," said Shakespeare, and that thought is at the heart of **cognitive therapy**. It helps the depressed person to become aware of the negative beliefs fuelling *emotional* introspections and, by challenging them *rationally*, reduces them. It is a very popular therapy because of its proven efficacy and suits many people. Unfortunately, formal cognitive therapy is expensive and slow with depressed people, often taking up to 20 sessions to stop the emotional introspections.

A common reason for people sinking into clinical depression is that they are in a deteriorating relationship at home or work which they endlessly introspect about. For them **interpersonal therapy** can be powerfully effective.

Depression destroys relationships because, when people around the depressed person find that they are beginning to feel depressed *themselves*, they pull away and emotionally disengage to protect themselves. This further isolates the individual who succumbs to even deeper levels of misery. Focusing on improving current relationships can be highly beneficial.[44] Interpersonal therapists work by improving the quality of people's relationships in people's lives now. Depression may be triggered off by one's reaction to a failing relationship, but even if one's relationship was good to start with, depression can rapidly deteriorate it. Interpersonal therapists may work by teaching social skills – how to ask questions, how to take an interest in other people, how to converse and think about other people's needs. All this helps reduce introspection and normalise sleep patterns.

When depression is caused by bereavement, interpersonal therapists help people recover from pathological responses by breaking the trance state of grieving and getting the bereaved person to re-engage with life.

Manic depression or bipolar disorder

It is generally agreed that manic depression has a significant genetic contribution to its genesis. It occurs with equal frequency in men and women and is usually treated with drugs, particularly lithium, which can help regulate the emotional seesaw that propels the sufferer from mania – extreme excitement and sometimes even violence – to depression – pure inertia and lassitude.

Manic depression occurs in a variety of profiles with some people visiting the depressed pole more frequently, and others spending more time in the manic pole. Some may cycle through both poles with dizzying rapidity.

It is also increasingly being recognised that self-management of the disorder, combined with medication, is the most effective treatment for the majority of patients. The skills to treat depression that we describe in this monograph are just as relevant for helping the manic depression sufferer stay out of depression.

When the manic pole is threatening it is important for the person to reduce stimulation, cut down on caffeine for example, and apply relaxation techniques. What is especially important is that the patient gets a good night's sleep. However exciting life may seem to the patient during the manic phase, unless they get enough REM sleep they will raise their arousal level, accelerating the onset of mania.

Manic depression in many ways highlights the role of black and white thinking in the genesis of depression. In the depressive phase the world is seen from a very black, pessimistic perspective indeed, whilst the opposite is true in the manic phase. Optimism and pessimism are two sides of the same coin. Just as runaway inflation is followed by recession in the world of economics, unbridled optimism is likely to trigger a pessimistic, depressive fallout when the unrealistic dreams turn into the ashes of disappointment.

Perhaps because of the genetic contribution the relationship between black and white thinking is more starkly isolated in manic depression. Black and white thinking is, as we have seen, the primitive thinking style of the emotional brain. The neocortex has evolved to enable us to refine that dichotomous style of thought so that we can perceive the myriad shades of grey between these two poles and thus chart a more flexible and realistic way through life's difficulties, giving us along the way the bonus of the possibility for ever higher development. Again we can see that the pre-condition for the ability to see the complexity of life and to navigate our way safely through it, is *less emotional arousal*.

From this understanding we can see that the therapeutic techniques deriving from an understanding of the human givens will be very useful in the treatment of bipolar disorder. We have ourselves encountered a number of clients who are successfully managing their condition using such techniques themselves without needing drug treatment, although we would wish to emphasise that the majority of patients will probably benefit most from a combination of drugs and human givens therapy.

The most effective way to lift depression

With a clearer understanding of what depression is, and what causes it, we can lift it more rapidly. The main task in any counselling for depression is simply to lower the emotional arousal and stop the negative emotional introspections in the patient as quickly as possible by any means at our disposal. This is done by drawing on all the human givens in realistic ways. That is why **human givens therapy** is the most effective form of therapy for depression and all other emotional disorders. We routinely find that, if you use *all* available approaches in one session, progress is much faster.

The human givens therapist, as well as integrating behavioural, cognitive and interpersonal approaches, also uses, for example, relaxation to calm the emotions before attempting other interventions, and works with the imaginative faculty to motivate people and help them change, solve problems and raise their self-esteem. We can use humour to demonstrate that life is not a black and white affair. We can flatter, inform, get patients to exercise, raise their curiosity and so on. In this way we have a truly organic mind/body approach – which is what human givens therapy is and can bring about the remission of depression in a fraction of the time that cognitive, behavioural or interpersonal therapy can individually. Human givens therapists routinely find that they can lift people out of the depressed state in just a handful of sessions, sometimes in one.[45] Clients quickly work to reduce negative introspections when it is explained to them that this is the mechanism that is generating their depression.

A delightful and deservedly famous example of a one session cure for depression comes from the widely documented work of the American clinician Milton H. Erickson, regarded by many as the twentieth century's most significant figure in psychotherapy.[46] It is easy to see from this case history how he worked spontaneously and naturally with the human givens.

The African Violet Queen of Milwaukee

In the middle of the last century one of Erickson's patients asked him to visit his aunt, a middle-aged spinster living in Milwaukee, USA. She was an independently wealthy woman with a housekeeper, maid and gardener who did everything for her, but she had fallen out with her family and for nine months had been horribly depressed.

Erickson called on her one evening. The housekeeper and the maid had left for the day. He identified himself very clearly as a doctor. "She was very passive," said Erickson, "and I demanded a tour of her home. She was sufficiently passive to permit me to have a guided tour. She led me from room to room. I looked around very carefully at everything. In the sun room I saw three beautiful African violets of different colours in full bloom, and a potting pot in which she was propagating another African violet. African violets are very delicate plants. They are easily killed by the slightest amount of neglect."

Erickson also noted from her large open Bible and from certain magazines lying around that she had a keen interest in the church. He then challenged the genuineness of her faith because she wasn't using her God given gifts in the way she should. This got her attention.

Then he said, "I'm going to give you some medical orders, and I want them carried out. Do you understand that? Will you agree that you will carry them out?" She passively agreed. Then he said, "Tomorrow you send your housekeeper to a nursery or a florist and you get African violets of all different hues. Those will be *your* African violets and you are going to take good care of them. That's a medical order.

"Then you tell your housekeeper to purchase 200 gift flower pots and 50 potting pots and enough potting soil. I want you to break off a leaf from each of your African violets and plant it in potting pots and grow additional African violets until they are mature plants. (These particular flowers propagate by planting the leaf.)

"And when you have an adequate supply of African violets, I want you to send one to every baby that's born in any family in your church. I want you to be a good Christian and send an African violet to the family of every baby christened in your church. I want you to send a gift of an African violet to everyone who is sick in your church. When a girl announces her engagement, I want you to send her an African violet. When people get married, I want you to send them African violets. In cases of death, you send a condolence card with an African violet. And the church bazaars – contribute a dozen or a score of African violets for sale."

With that Erickson left. It was soon reported that her depression had lifted. As Erickson said years later, "Anybody that takes care of that many African violets is too busy to be depressed. She died in her seventies and I have a newspaper cutting recording the fact that, 'The African Violet Queen of Milwaukee has died'. I saw her only once."

We can see clearly from this case history many of the principles of human givens therapy. First Erickson quickly assessed what needs were unfulfilled in her life. Then he focused her attention and made her promise to do something that he knew would re-engage her with the community. He creatively drew on her own belief system and resources. In this case it was her skill with African violets which he cleverly connected to the universal appreciation the human community has for flowers. He gave her enough work to do to ensure her negative introspections would stop and her depression would lift. In other words he devised a therapy specifically for her, one that she could keep up independently.

This last point is a particularly important one. Therapists have to help depressed people use whatever skills they have to reconnect them to the community so that their needs can be met autonomously. If they haven't got the skills the therapist has to teach them or make sure that someone else does. If they don't start to generate the fulfilment of their needs from the environment under their own steam they will relapse into clinical depression again. It's inevitable. Human givens cannot be ignored.

The above often cited example of one session, solution focused therapy for depression can be added to many times over, not only from the work of Erickson but from well recorded cases back in history and from the current workload of many brilliant brief therapists working today.

Sometimes it can be difficult for counsellors, GPs or social workers with a caseload of clinically depressed patients with a tremendous number of social problems in their lives – debts, redundancy, no work, accidents, family break-up, illness, being bullied, being a single mother – to see how to apply the principles contained in this paper.

The key point to remember when a depressed person's problems seem to be located so firmly in the environment is that there is no situation in life that is so difficult that other people haven't already traversed it, or are going through it now, and managing to cope *without* getting clinically depressed.[47] Clinical depression is an additional layer of suffering on what is already a difficult situation for a person.

To take an extreme example, imagine two patients dying of cancer side by side in a hospital, one of them in a state of clinical depression and the other not. The depressed patient has merely added an *additional* layer of suffering on top of his life situation. The patient who is *not* depressed will still be actively engaged with life: solving problems, looking forward to visits from relatives, organising the disposal of their estate, designing their funeral service and generally setting short term goals that can be accomplished in what time they have left.

The depressed patient, meanwhile, will be indulging in frightening themselves, emotionally introspecting, and, as a consequence of negative introspection, which reduces serotonin levels in the brain, actually experiencing more physical pain in their dying. (This is because one of the functions of serotonin is to modulate pain responses.)

When counselling depressed people whose real life circumstances are hard, it is essential to get them focused on solving their problems by breaking those problems down into manageable chunks, and to work alongside them finding practical ways in which to do so. This may, for example, involve helping them to renegotiate debt repayments or coordinate social services, or showing them how to avail themselves of care relief services. It's a two-pronged approach. One is to actively help them solve the environmental problems and the other is to lower their arousal level and stop them negatively introspecting about their circumstances. The best way to do this is invariably to focus their attention outwards into problem solving.

Postnatal depression is caused by emotionally arousing introspections, as in all other depressions. It is not different except that the depressive is also responsible for a baby.

Comorbidity

Once depression is lifted some additional psychological repair work may still need to be done. People are often lonely because they don't have the skills for making small talk and have not learnt how to make natural, easy contact with other human beings. They may need to practise other social skills or learn how to job hunt, or prepare for a change of career, all of which are possible once the depression is lifted and the person can think again. We should never forget that emotional arousal hijacks our thinking brain and drastically limits our options, not only for thought, but also for action. Once arousal levels are lowered most people can get on with their lives.

But some people seem to get more than their fair share of bad things happening to them. This often happens, not only because they have the pessimistic, emotional black and white thinking style, but because they also have some additional vulnerability. Depression is often accompanied by other conditions and this is called comorbidity.

Comorbidity simply means the simultaneous existence of two or more disorders, whether physical or psychological, and there are often simultaneous syndromes or disorders present in the depressed person. These range from anxiety disorders such as panic attacks and OCD, medical conditions and personality disorders.

Addictive behaviour is found in some depressed people because, having become depressed, they turn to drugs or alcohol as a way of trying to lift their mood. They then, of course, end up with two problems.

All addicts, whether initially depressed or not, eventually become depressed because so many of their needs are unfulfilled.

Panic attacks often present with depression. The counsellor must know how to reassure a sufferer that there is nothing organically wrong and that their symptoms are in fact those of a fear reaction – inappropriate firing of the fight or flight response. Normalising the event and taking the fear out of it will result in their introspecting about it less. Then they should be shown how to bring the anxiety under control by, for example, learning how to stop panic breathing.

The experience of sexual or physical abuse, a serious road accident, or extreme violence, may result in post traumatic stress disorder (PTSD). It will inevitably lead to depression if untreated. This is because traumatised people endlessly introspect about the traumatic event and their subsequent uncontrolled responses to it. Many have had their depression lifted in one session by means of the fast phobia cure.[48]

Effective counsellors and psychotherapists (there is no meaningful difference between the two titles, both need to be equally competent at relieving clients of their psychological/ behavioural distress as quickly as possible) require a range of skills that let them operate creatively, in a comprehensive, holistic way, treating each patient as an individual who has unique beliefs, resources and abilities. Human givens therapy is a package of skills that brings together all the knowledge and techniques from many different disciplines in the service of relieving distress. We believe that training counsellors and psychotherapists in this approach is the most practical and cost effective way forward in this hitherto confusing field, not only for the treatment of clinical depression but for all other forms of emotional disorder.

Taking the wrong road

The adverse effects of too much introspecting which we have been describing explains why 'insight' therapy can often do so much harm. A lady in her early 40s, well dressed, tall and attractive, came to see one of us (JG) recently. She'd been attending various psychotherapists over the past two years and was referred to me by a body therapist whom she had started to consult, in some desperation, to relieve her misery. She said her confidence had completely collapsed to the degree that, were she to meet a friend in the street, even whilst talking to her, she would introspect about what kind of an impression she was making and worry about this excessively.

At work, if she were talking to a customer, she would find herself becoming acutely self conscious, getting tongue-tied and befuddled with the customer.

As she was quite clear that this problem had been getting worse over the past two years I pointed out that it might not be a coincidence that the more counselling she had had the more her problems seemed to have got worse. She agreed.

She and her husband had worked hard together and made a great success of a restaurant in Galway. When she had enough money and spare time she decided to "work on herself" and enter counselling to "develop her potential". At that point she was not depressed but, she said, the counselling made her realise that she had had problems all her life, they went back to her childhood and her relationship with her alcoholic father. She now felt she had been "in denial" of those painful feelings until she started attending therapists who helped her to get in touch with this suppressed pain which was now coming out.

Now this is a pattern we come across time and time again in clinical practice. Clients attending psychodynamic counsellors become emotionally dysfunctional. Using the language of 'therapy speak' they access more and more emotional pain, their intelligence drops because of the emotional arousal until they will even accept the twisted logic that says *you have to become more dysfunctional before you can get better!*

This logic would be rejected in any other area of life. If, for example, you went to the doctor with a stomach ulcer and he gave you some treatment and the pain got worse and he examined you again and said, "I can see what's happening. The treatment is really working. Before you came to see me your immune system was repressing cancer. It is now no longer repressing it. And, as a result of my treatment, we are making progress, the painful cancer is growing!"

Clearly that would be utterly absurd.

And yet such reasoning is followed, in all innocence, by many therapists who damage their patients in the process.

By contrast, for a human givens therapist it is axiomatic

that, if the client is emotionally distressed and disturbed, the reason is because their needs are not being met *now* or that they are misusing the tools that nature gave them to get those needs met. They need coaching to correct this.

In this case I immediately directed the therapy towards finding out what needs were not being fulfilled in this woman's life. I asked her about her children – they seemed to be growing up normally with no more than the usual problems that parents encounter with a young family. She had no money worries. But, when I asked about her relationship with her husband, she readily admitted that this had been deteriorating at an alarming rate. In fact, they had arranged to meet a mediator the following week to negotiate a separation. They had stopped sharing a bedroom some months ago.

Curiously, this was a subject she didn't even bring up until I questioned her. Instead she had been asking me whether I could help her to "get in touch with her past" because there *must* be something there, perhaps in her relationship with her father, and she felt if she could uncover this it would release her from her lack of confidence. In other words, she was asking me for more of the same kind of emotionally arousing therapy which had caused her problems.

Perhaps one of the most worrying aspects of this case is that this woman wasn't particularly psychologically troubled prior to going to counselling. In fact, as she and her husband built their very successful business together, they didn't have any marriage problems.

It was only as the business became more successful and she had more time on her hands that she decided to do some work on personal development and have counselling to do so. It was in this context that the marital problems started and she began to become emotionally dysfunctional.

To be of use to this woman I had to undo the effects of the

'counselling' she had undergone and help her get her needs met, perhaps by helping her rebuild her relationship with her husband which would certainly lower her emotional distress. My first step in this case, therefore, was to arrange to see both of them together to see whether or not there was a possibility of salvaging the relationship.

An avoidable death

A woman recently told one of us (JG) about the circumstances of her husband's death. She had been deeply worried about his depressed state and felt he was at risk of suicide. She finally managed to persuade her husband to see his GP, although he felt it was pointless to do so. But, having got him to the surgery, all the GP did was change his antidepressant medication. This meant that any benefit he might have been getting from his previous antidepressant would diminish while the new antidepressant would take some weeks to start working.

This is absolutely the wrong way to treat depressives who are contemplating suicide, as many of them do. A doctor needs to act there and then to lift the person's mood. Had the GP worked from a human givens perspective he would have known how to challenge the man's attributional style, curb his introspections, create a positive expectancy and buy crucial time by making him promise not to kill himself yet.

The man was obviously highly emotionally aroused and, if the GP had known how to use guided imagery, he could have quickly lowered his arousal level, focused his attention, and taught him how to calm himself down and relax. Then the doctor could have helped him to see his situation more clearly. He could make positive statements, such as, "Depression is not a permanent state and yours will very probably remit. It does so naturally in the majority of cases." He could have made him laugh or helped him decide on a course of action. He could have reminded him about things that he had achieved in his life and of his proven ability to make changes happen, thus raising his self-esteem. The man would then have left that GP's surgery believing that change was possible, having had it actually demonstrated to him. In twenty minutes he could have been calmed and reassured.

But the GP's failure to realise the seriousness of the situation, and the importance of creating hopefulness in his patient, meant that the man went out and hanged himself – the woman lost her husband and his children lost their father.

Unfortunately, this is happening over and over again because of the mistreatment of depression. Nearly twice as many people commit suicide as die on the roads, and nine times more attempt suicide. Although women are two to three times more likely to suffer depression than men, men are three times more likely to kill themselves. This, again, is due to emotional arousal affecting thinking styles. Women tend to dwell endlessly on their emotions while men tend to go into 'problem solving' mode to deal with problems. A black and white thinking-style male sees suicide as a solution to a problem. And, because males tend to be more action orientated than females, they are more likely to carry out the 'solution'.

The most sensible way to lower depression and suicide rates is to spread accurate information among the general public about what depression is – an emotion that stimulates black and white thinking and introspection – and train sufficient members of the caring professions in the techniques for lifting it quickly, working from the human givens perspective. These techniques include calming a depressed person down quickly; finding out what needs are not being fulfilled in their life; raising their self esteem; identifying and challenging their attributional thinking style; and demonstrating, from the very first session, that change is possible – thus creating a sense of positive expectancy and a belief in, and will to, change.

The following case histories are typical of this approach and show how the use of such skills can be incorporated in counselling sessions.

Effective therapy: casebook examples

The widow

Mary, in her late sixties, was physically robust but her face was etched with grief and despair. Her husband Tom, who had been the mainstay of her life, had died six months earlier. Mary was still tortured by images of his final suffering. She couldn't sleep at night and yet lay on her bed until lunch time because she saw no point in getting up. She was also scared to leave the house because of the panic attacks she had been suffering since Tom's death.

After listening to her story, I explained the importance of relaxation and how to control her panic attacks. With guided imagery and progressive muscle relaxation she slowed down her breathing, lines of tension eased from her face and, with eyes closed, she gratefully sank back into the comfort of the armchair. I then quietly suggested that she could let go of the image of her husband's final suffering and recall instead happy images of their time together. I gave her time to do this and she clearly enjoyed it. I reminded her of the many strengths and skills she had developed in raising her large family, now scattered around the world. I also told her that what her husband would most want from her now was to call upon that strength, and the strength of her relationship with him, to face the new challenges in her life.

When she opened her eyes we worked out a plan together for what she would do each day, starting with what time she would get up. She said she would like to start baking again so we built that into the plan. I explained the importance of aerobic exercise in keeping down her stress levels and lifting depressed feelings. She agreed to resume walking with her neighbour in the evenings, which she had stopped doing since her Tom had died. To ensure that her need for human company would be met I persuaded her to join a social craft group in the town.

Over the next few weeks her mood lifted. As she became physically active again she took on more jobs around the house, including some decorating and gardening. Very soon after this her son in America sent her a ticket to join him for a holiday over there. When she was depressed, he had withdrawn from her and had been reluctant to invite her over. But now that she was focused outward again he was happy to see her, which lifted her spirits still further.

The effect of the human givens approach in this case was rapid and straightforward, as it so often is.

Mary was first helped to bring down her emotional arousal in order to free her to see reality in a more empowering way. Then the meaning of Tom's death and love was reframed into a challenge to her to move on in her life. She was given back a sense of control over her panic attacks. Pleasure and challenge was brought back into her life by resuming walking with friends, baking and decorating. The satisfaction of her needs for attention was shifted from me, her therapist, to her local community, by getting her to join a local craft group. Finally the lifting of her depression brought her into closer contact with her family again.

The suicide attempt

Judith, a woman in her late twenties, was married with no children and living in rural England.

She came to see me (JG) following her discharge from hospital after treatment for a twenty-inch diagonal wound across her chest inflicted in her attempted suicide. The stabbing had been so severe that she had been kept in hospital for a week. She had made this attempt on her life because her problems seemed so large and numerous that she could see no other way out.

Judith showed the common risk factor for depression already referred to: black and white global thinking – the tendency to see the forest but not the individual trees nor the various paths in it. To use another metaphor, if we hold a stone up to our eyes all we can see is the stone. The rest of the world is blotted out as surely as if the stone were as large as a mountain. For a global thinker the little stone becomes the universe.

The global thinker tends to focus so much on their problems that they can see no way around or through them. All that exists are their problems. They inevitably lose a sense of proportion about their situation. Difficulties become catastrophes. Their imagination piles up the problems one on top of another so that a mountain of misery completely blocks out the wider view. This is exactly the process that led Judith to her desperate act of attempted self annihilation.

This was her story. She had been unemployed for three years since injuring her back in an accident at work. She was currently waiting for a claim for legal damages to be heard by the courts. Shortly before her attempted suicide she read in the paper about a person who had lost their injuries claim against their employer, and was forced to sell the family home to pay their employer's legal costs. Judith was terrified that if she lost her legal action she and her husband might become homeless too. They were just, in fact, in the process of having a new house built and that was one more thing that troubled Judith ... it had fallen behind schedule. "The builders are taking us to the cleaners", she said. "The house will *never* be finished. The site is a *complete* mess." Again, pessimism and black and white thinking.

Judith also had a phobia about dogs. Her neighbours had a dog and, unless her husband was with her, she was scared to pass their house. This meant that, for much of her time, she was effectively trapped in her own home.

Judith was additionally much troubled by the fact that her sister, whom she was close to, and was in counselling, had recently announced that, as a child, she had been sexually abused by their father. Her sister expected and wanted her support. But Judith also had a very close relationship with her father who vehemently denied the abuse. Naturally her father also wanted and expected her support. She didn't know what to do.

Here we again see black and white thinking at work. Black and white thinking creates a low tolerance for the inevitable ambiguities of life. So much of life is full of unknowns, certainty is the exception. We can't know for sure, for example, that we are choosing the right career, the right partner, the right house, or even the best holiday. In life we can't always know for sure why what happens happens. There are too many contributing factors. Someone might say, for example, "Why is my son a drug addict? Is it because I wasn't sufficiently firm with him? Maybe I didn't show him enough love. But then, why isn't my other son a drug addict? I didn't show favouritism to either son. Maybe it's his genes? Or is it the company he keeps? Perhaps it was his disappointment in a love affair that made him vulnerable!" Maybe it was all or none of these reasons.

Black and white thinking demands a definite answer to every ambiguous life situation. Judith's thinking style demanded that she unambiguously support *either* her father *or* her sister. But she loved them both so she was paralysed by her continual analytical introspections of the situation.

In the first session with Judith I used about 25 minutes of the session to get her to relax using guided imagery. I then removed her dog phobia. (Phobias are easily cured in the vast majority of cases in a single session using the technique already mentioned called the 'fast phobia cure'. By using physical relaxation, with a particular form of guided imagery, the client's anxiety reaction to the phobic stimuli is totally desensitised.)

Whilst she was still relaxed we discussed and reframed the other three main problems she was worrying about. I asked her what evidence she had that she was going to lose her court case. She repeated the story in the newspaper.

"That could be a completely different case from your's," I told her. "We must concentrate on the specific evidence. What does your barrister say is the likely outcome of *your* case?"

"Well, he says that I am certain to win since I was injured at work and there are sworn statements from other workers who were witnesses. All that remains to be decided, according to him, is how much in damages I receive."

I helped her to see that she was misusing her imagination by creating an improbable negative outcome to her court case. The idea that she was facing the loss of the family home was entirely unreasonable and, because she was relaxed and could think straight, she agreed this was so.

We next considered the problem of the alleged sexual abuse of her sister by their father. It was clear that there was no external, validating evidence that abuse had taken place. Judith herself had never seen or experienced such abuse. In such circumstances the only reasonable course of action was to tolerate the ambiguity of not knowing what had actually happened, if anything had. Her sister's memories might be true or yet again they might be an artifact – illusory memories – created by the type of counselling she was receiving. I explained that, at present, there was no way of knowing either way for sure. In any case it wasn't her problem. Her father and sister were going to have to find a way of dealing with it themselves. Judith gave a huge sigh of relief when she realised she didn't have to solve the problem. She could offer her love and support to both family members – at least until more objective evidence became available.

Finally we considered her problem about her new home. What did the architect supervising the building programme have to say? "Well, according to him", she said, "we are only six months behind schedule." I joked with her that six months behind schedule was equivalent to twelve months ahead of schedule as far as the average builder was concerned!

When Judith came back to see me the following week she was no longer depressed. Indeed, she had been out on her own and cycled past the house with the dog without experiencing a panic attack. She declared herself baffled by how she could ever have got things so much out of proportion. But of course we now know why she did. It was due to her attributional style. Her global thinking style, combined with black and white thinking and endless introspecting, formed the toxic brew that maintained the emotion of clinical depression and created her suicidal impulses.

The crying woman

I (IT) saw Susan five years ago when her husband brought her to me at her GP's suggestion. Her heavy figure oozed misery and seemed to suck the energy out of everyone around her. Speaking with reluctance, it was all such an effort, she told me her history whilst tears slowly ran down her face: eleven years of severe depression, three serious suicide attempts, hospitalisation, psychiatrists, antidepressants that hadn't worked, psychotherapy that made her feel even worse, "if that was possible". And now she was talking again about ending it all. "What is the point of living?"

Following the golden rule of not taking too much history with depressed people but showing the client instead that things can be different *in the first session*, after 30 minutes I set to work. She looked such a picture of despair that, on an impulse, I decided to use humour, an age-old and valuable way to help people see how they are exaggerating things. This need not mean telling jokes or being witty. I simply drew on her own resources and asked her what made her laugh?

Back came the inevitable slow monotone response, "Nothing makes me laugh."

"I don't believe you."

"I never laugh."

"*Everyone* has a sense of humour."

"I have no sense of humour. I *never* laugh."

So deep in her depression trance was Susan that I almost believed her, but I carried on anyway and asked her to do an experiment. "Just close your eyes and let your mind go back to the last time you had tears of laughter rolling down your face."

She obediently closed her eyes and I sat back and waited, fingers crossed, while her brain went on a search. Within a few minutes she started to smile. The smiles turned to laughter.

Then she started to cry, but this time with tears of laughter! She opened her eyes and splutteringly told me what she had remembered that was so funny. The laughter had dissipated her depression, puncturing a hole in the global blanket of misery she had held fast around her.

For a while at least her brain was working and we talked normally. I asked her what she most regretted about her depression and she said it was the fact that for twelve years, since her "illness", she and her husband had not been on a holiday and she felt this was so unfair on her husband because, when they were young, holidays had meant a lot to them and he still wanted to see more of the world. As, it turned out, so did she.

I called the husband in. He was astonished and pleased to see her smiling and so changed. Whilst in this positive, lively state I got them to both promise, as part of the treatment, to book a holiday straight away to somewhere they really wanted to go but where they had never been before.

I had to see Susan eleven times in all before I was sure she was out of depression. (Coincidentally, once for every year she had been depressed.) At first she would come in and say she was just as bad as before – black and white thinking again – but, by getting her to scale her changing moods and achievements and teaching her how to change her attributional style, I got her out of depression. Scaling the gradual remission of symptoms is a powerful tool of therapy precisely because it is *not* all or nothing. It is a technique drawn from solution focused brief therapy in which, for instance, a client is asked to place themselves on a scale where 0 means no change in mood and 10 represents a completely positive and optimistic mood. It is a practical and motivating means of monitoring gradual upward changes.

The holiday of course gave Susan something outside herself

to focus on. They chose to go to Australia. It brought their relationship back to life; it brought planning, excitement and new experiences into their lives. I have since had several postcards from Susan and her husband from various parts of the world. She is enjoying life now.

Part of the reason people cannot initiate such activity themselves when they are depressed is that they cannot easily make connections when they are emotionally aroused – the emotional arousal stops them thinking clearly. They just can't see the bigger picture.

Heart attack!

Dr Michael Yapko tells of a deeply depressed, anxious and exhausted man who had had a heart attack. Since his recovery he had become so focused on his conviction that he was going to die that he wasn't willing to listen to anyone about anything else. Yapko devised a simple behavioural strategy to break the deep trance state the man was in. He persuaded him to call out to his wife every fifteen minutes, throughout the day and night from wherever he was in the house, "I am still alive!"

Eventually, by just saying to himself, "I am still alive, I am still alive" over and over again, it suddenly dawned on him that, "My God! I *am* alive!"

That was the turning point. He came out of his depression.

* * * * *

THE IMPORTANCE of the findings in this monograph are hard to overstate, especially in the light of the discoveries being made about the dangers of antidepressant drugs, even the modern ones like the 'Prozac group' of SSRIs. The problems with these drugs are described by Dr Joseph Glenmullen of Harvard Medical School in his book, *Prozac Backlash*.[49] Antidepressants are very powerful and interfere with the mind/body system in multiple ways which can cause dizziness, nausea, anxiety disorders, facial and whole body tics, major muscle spasms, parkinsonism (symptoms similar to those seen in Parkinson's disease), brain damage, sexual dysfunction (in up to 60% of the people who take them), memory loss, neurotoxicity and debilitating withdrawal symptoms that are often mistaken for the original symptoms returning but can be even more severe. There is also a direct link between suicide and violent behaviour and taking them.

Despite these dangers antidepressants are often given, not only to otherwise healthy people but to children whose brains are still forming (human frontal lobe connections are not fully in place until a person is about 20 years old.[50]) and to older people with early signs of brain deterioration.

Given this increasing recognition that antidepressants are much more dangerous than their promoters had hoped, the importance of the findings about the drawbacks of the simplistic medical model (which falsely maintains that 'depression is caused by a chemical imbalance in the brain'), and the significance of how the right type of psychotherapy is a much better treatment, we are entering a time of hope for sufferers. From now on, help for depressed patients should improve as more health workers come to understand the real basis for depression and receive training in effective psychotherapy approaches.

We can but stand back in awe at the complexity and sophistication of the human brain and marvel at how it has evolved to foster flexibility of thought and action instead of automatically reacting to stimuli in a mechanical way, as lesser animals do (and *we* still do when we become emotional).

But awe, too, is an emotion that can lock our attention and make us stupid. As we continue to evolve we struggle with the emotional chains that bind us with a power and primitive purpose that are a mystery to most of us. The cleverest of individuals can be swept along by anger, fear, greed, lust or depression. Fortunately, by looking at emotionally disturbed people through the human givens perspective, we can use our knowledge of what it means to be human to help those who temporarily lose their way.

* * * * *

Summary of the major new ideas in this monograph

• *Depression is essentially a REM sleep disorder*

We have known for some time that depressed people have a very high level of physiological arousal. We also know they do a lot of negative thinking (worrying). We know too that depressed people suffer from insomnia and other sleep disorders, have disturbed REM sleep and wake up exhausted unable to activate or motivate themselves. It is also known that both anti-depressants and certain forms of psychotherapy are often effective in lifting clinical depression. But there has never been a clear understanding that links all these facts. With the discovery of why we evolved to dream[51], however, we have the missing piece of the jigsaw puzzle that brings all this information together in one clear picture: a complete psychobiological explanation for clinical depression.

Dreaming is the means of discharging emotionally arousing introspections from the previous day that haven't been expressed. Depressed people are excessively negatively introspecting because of a failure to get their essential emotional needs met. Emotional arousal automatically forces the brain into a reactive, black and white mode of thinking, reducing its ability to think in more subtle, objective ways. So, after a setback, someone with an essentially pessimistic outlook will inevitably catastrophise their interpretations of life events and excessively introspect about these interpretations, which puts excessive pressure on the dreaming process and distorts the REM sleep system causing excessive autonomic arousal discharge, leading in turn to physical exhaustion and subsequent clinical depression.

We can now see that all therapies that are effective at lifting depression break this cycle. (All antidepressants reduce or normalise REM sleep. All effective psychotherapies break the negative introspection cycle and focus the client on solving problems and engaging with life again.)

- *The depressive's black and white thinking style is fuelled by the emotional brain's ancient response system*

The attributional style of a depressed person precisely echoes the reactive, all or nothing, response system in the brain: fight or flight, good or bad, love or hate, near or far.

- *Rapid eye movements (REM) are caused by the PGO wave triggering off the orientation response in the brain*

During REM sleep there is a massive firing of the PGO orientation response. The eyes dart about during REM sleep because they are trying, even though closed, to scan the environment in response to this. However the source of the arousal is internal: the non acted out introspections from the previous day.

The implications for lifting depression

- Depressed people are highly aroused, so in order to work with them cognitively, or in any way at all, it is first necessary to calm them down using any relaxation skills that are appropriate – breathing retraining, massage, guided imagery or relaxing hypnotic techniques.

- Stop emotional introspecting by whatever means. (Any therapy or counselling that encourages prolonged emotional introspection is toxic. This is because, firstly, emotional arousal makes us stupid and results in black and white thinking, and, secondly, because excessive arousal, resulting from negative emotional introspection, distorts the REM sleep mechanism and thereby leads us into clinical depression.)

- Focus clients' attention outwards: get them physically active (aerobic exercise), focus them on pleasurable activity, problem solving, challenging black and white thinking etc.

- Get clients to see how things could be different by actively using their imagination in a positive way with visualisation and guided imagery.

- Postnatal depression responds to the same principles.

- Antidepressants can be effective but carry many risks. The right type of counselling is often quicker in effect and greatly reduces the chances of future episodes of depression.

References

1. Seligman, M.E.P. (1990) *Learned Optimism*. New York, Pocket Books. After reviewing the data on the rise and rise of depression in Western countries psychologist Martin Seligman wrote, "We are in the midst of an epidemic of depression, one with consequences that, through suicides, takes as many lives as the AIDS epidemic and is more widespread. Severe depression is ten times more prevalent today than it was fifty years ago. It assaults women twice as often as men, and now it strikes a full decade earlier in life on average than it did a generation ago."

2. Lane, R. E., (2000) *The Loss of Happiness in Market Democracies*. Yale University Press.

3. UNICEF, (1993) *The Progress of Nations*. United Nations, 45.

4. Seligman in James Buie (1988) *'Me' Decades Generate Depression: Individualism Erodes Commitment to Others*. APA Monitor 19:18. "People born after 1945 were ten times more likely to suffer from depression than people born 50 years earlier."

5. *Medical Health Index,* 1999, IMS Health.

6. *The global burden of disease,* 1997, World Health Organisation.

7. Nemeroff, C.B. (1998) The neurobiology of depression. *Scientific American,* 278, 6, 28–35.

8. McGrath, E. *et al.* (1990) *Women and Depression*. American Psychological Association.

9. McGrath, E. *et al.* (1990) *Women and Depression*. American Psychological Association.

10. Griffin, J. and Tyrrell, I. (1998) *Hypnosis and Trance States: a new psychobiological explanation*. European Therapy Studies Institute.

11. Griffin, J. and Tyrrell, I. (1998) *Hypnosis and Trance States: a new psychobiological explanation*. European Therapy Studies Institute.

12. Golman, D. (1996) *Emotional Intelligence*. Bloomsbury Publishing, London.

13. Seligman in James Buie (1988) *'Me' Decades Generate Depression: Individualism Erodes Commitment to Others*. APA Monitor 19:18.
"On the whole, you do not find much in the way of depression as we know it – suicide, hopelessness, giving up, low self-esteem, passivity and the like – in nonwestern cultures ..."

14. Kleinman, A. (1995) *World Mental Health: Problems and Priorities in Low-Income Countries*. New York: Oxford University Press (for the United Nations).

15. Lloyd, D. and Rossi, E. (1992) *High Frequency Biological Rhythms: Function of the Ultradians*. New York: Springer-Verlag.

16. Rossi, E. and Nimmons, D. (1991) *The 20 Minute Break*. J. P. Tarcher, Inc.

17. "Those in low-status jobs with little control over their work got sick and died much more often than those in higher status jobs with more control." Finding from a study of 10,000 London civil servants reported in *Mind Sculpture* by Professor Ian Robertson, Bantam Press (1999).

18. Rutter, M. (1971) Parent-child separation: psychological effects on the children. *Journal of Child Psychology and Psychiatry*. 12, 233–60.

19. Richards, M. et al., (1997) The effects of divorce and separation on mental health in a national UK birth cohort. *Psychological Medicine, 27*, 1121–8.

20. McLanahan, S. and Sandefur, G. (1994) *Growing Up with a Single Parent*. Harvard University Press. See also Angel, R and Angel, J. (1993) *Painful Inheritance: Health and the New Generation of Fatherless Families*. University of Wisconsin Press. See also Amato, P. and Booth, A. (1997) *A Generation at Risk*. Also, Forehand, R. et al. (1997) Is Adolescent Adjustment Following Parental Divorce a Function of Predivorce Adjustment? *Journal of Abnormal Child Psychology.*

21. Papermaster, D. (1995) Necessary but Insufficient. *Nature Medicine*. Vol. 1 874–5. See also Le Fanu. J. (1999) *The Rise and Fall of Modern Medicine*. Little Brown and Company (UK)

22. Yapko, M.D. (1997) *Breaking the Patterns of Depression*. Doubleday

23. Danton, W. Antonuccio, D. and DeNelsky, G. (1995). Depression: psychotherapy is the best medicine. *Professional Psychology Research and Practice, 26,* 574.

24. *Diagnostic and Statistical Manual of Mental Disorders* (4th ed.) (1994). Washington D.C. American Psychiatric Association.

25. *Diagnosis, Vol. 2 Treatment Aspect,* United States Public Health, Service Agency.

26. Of course psychodynamic therapy can, in its early stages, be helpful to some people. We all experience being troubled and worried about things and finding it helpful to talk about our problem with a friend. And, provided the friend is sympathetic, it can create a space wherein we can review what we are worried about and maybe get new perspectives on our problems. And that can be very helpful as long as the conversations are focusing on current problems. It is part of the way we deal with difficulties. But when counselling relationships turns to resurrecting everything that has gone wrong in clients' lives – encouraging them to get emotional about it – that tends to make people dysfunctional.

This is the reason why psychodynamic counsellors have such problems around their concept of 'counter transference' where the therapist gets emotionally involved with the client and finds that 'stuff' from *their* own past keeps coming up all the time. Then they have to go for supervision talk this through to try and 'understand' it. But the reason this happens is that the therapists themselves have undergone a process of making their own emotional reaction patterns hyper-aroused and easily triggered off, misusing what is, in limited doses, a useful tool.

27. Dubovsky, S.L. (1997) *Mind-Body Deceptions: the psychosomatics of everyday life*. W.W. Norton and Co.

28. Robinson, I. (1999) *Mind Sculpture*. Bantam Press

29. Linde, K., Ramirex, G., Mulrow, C.D., Pauls, A., Weidenhammer, W., Melchart, D. (1996) St John's Wort for Depression: an overview and meta-analysis of randomized clinical trials. *British Medical Journal*, 313, 253–258.

30. There are numerous anecdotal references to the effectiveness of St John's wort for insomnia but no scientific studies have been done that we can trace. It is important to remember that sleep difficulties are a cardinal symptom of depression. These difficulties may take the form of having trouble falling asleep, tossing and turning or sleeping fitfully, or waking up too early in the morning. So distressing are such symptoms that they may overwhelm the clinical picture and the depressed person may misdiagnose the condition as insomnia.

31. Rosenthal, N. (1998) *St John's Wort*. Thornsens.

32. Danton, W. Antonuccio, D. and DeNelsky, G. (1995) Depression: psychotherapy is the best medicine. *Professional Psychology Research and Practice*, 26, 574.

33. Griffin, J. and Tyrrell, I. (1999) *Psychotherapy and the Human Givens*. European Therapy Studies Institute.

34. Griffin, J. (1997) *The Origin of Dreams*. The Therapist Ltd.

35. Vogel, G.W. (1979) *The Function of Sleep*. Drucker-Collins *et al.* (eds.), 233–250. Academic Press, New York.

36. Nemeroff, C.B. (1998) The neurobiology of depression. *Scientific American*. 278, 6, 28–35.

37. Danton, W. Antonuccio, D. and DeNelsky, G. (1995) Depression: psychotherapy is the best medicine. *Professional Psychology Research and Practice*, 26, 574.

38. Peterson, C. and Seligman, M.E.P. Causal explanations as a factor for depression: theory and evidence. *Psychological Review*, 91, 341–74

39. Yapko, M.D. (1999) *Hand-Me-Down Blues: how to stop depression spreading in families*. Doubleday.

40. Howard Burton et al., (1986) The relationship of depression to survival in chronic renal failure, *Psychosomatic Medicine*.

41. Martin, P. (1997) *The Sickening Mind: brain, behaviour, immunity and disease*. Harper Collins.

42 "The efficacy of antidepressent activity, accross drugs, is directly related to the capacity of drugs to produce large and sustained reductions of REM sleep." Ellman, S. J. and Antrobus, J. S. eds. (1991 2nd edition) *The Mind in Sleep*. John Wiley.

43. Dolnick, E. (1998) *Madness on the Couch*. Simon & Schuster.

44. Allen, N.H.P. and Burns, A. (1995) The non-cognitive features of dementia. *Reviews in Clinical Gerontology,* 5,57–75. "Having a wide range of social roles is known to act as a buffer against the effects of life events that can otherwise lead to depression."

45. Anon. (2000) For an example of the client's viewpoint on being helped out of depression quickly with the human givens approach see, On the receiving end ... *The New Therapist,* 7, 3.

46. Zeig, J.K. and Munion, W.M. (1999) *Milton H. Erickson.* Sage.

47. Elwick, L. (1999) A Headache to end all headaches. *The Therapist, 6, 3.* This is a poignant description by a woman who, from being healthy and fit, suffered a transpontine infarction resulting in sudden total paralysis and locked-in syndrome. Over several years she found ways to communicate again during which her sense of awareness and intelligence remained undimmed. Throughout this ordeal she did not suffer from clinical depression.

48. This core technique is used by human givens counsellors and therapists to remove phobias (any type) and detraumatise PTSD responses. Essentially it transforms an emotionally conditioned memory seated in the limbic system into a normal memory available to the higher cortex. For single event trauma accident, violent attack, rape, heart attack etc. – the process takes one session.

49. Glenmullen, J. (2001) *Prozac Backlash.* Simon & Schuster.

50. Robinson, I. (1999) *Mind Sculpture.* Bantam Press.

51. Griffin, J. (1997). *The Origin of Dreams.* The Therapist Ltd.

About the authors

JOE GRIFFIN is a psychologist with a thriving psychotherapy practice. Over the last decade thousands of health professionals have enjoyed his practical workshops and seminars on effective psychotherapy and counselling. He is widely recognised as one of the most informed and entertaining speakers on the subject having studied with many of the leading figures of the psychotherapy world. He is also a scientist and spent 12 years researching why animals and humans evolved to dream. The resulting book, *The Origin of Dreams,* offered the first holistic synthesis – a recognition of the interdependence of the biological and the psychological – to explain the origin, function and meaning of dreams. His findings about mental processes have been described by scientific reviewers as, "the key to all psychic states ... an important milestone ... moves our understanding on significantly ... a watershed in our exploration of the evolution of mental processes." He has also published a new theory to explain autism and is currently writing a book on the practical application of the human givens approach to counselling.

IVAN TYRRELL is a psychotherapist (specialising in brief therapy for depression and anxiety disorders) and a writer with a particular interest in the psychology of perception. He is a founder member of the European Therapy Studies Institute (ETSI) which, in 1992, launched *The New Therapist* – the popular multi-disciplinary magazine for all caring professionals. His work for *The New Therapist* (now called *Human Givens: radical psychology today*) involves him in a continuing programme of writing, interviewing, and investigating the latest developments in psychology, psychotherapy and the study of human behaviour. He lectures at educational and medical institutions throughout the UK. The *British Medical Journal* said of his book, *The Survival Option,* published by Jonathan Cape, "his practical information is reliable", and *The Times* wrote that it contained, "facts, not emotion... should be in every home in the country." Both he and Joe Griffin are members of the group involved with developing the human givens approach to applying scientific knowledge of human psychology and behaviour to psychotherapy and counselling.